CRITERIA

a One-Man Comic Sci-fi Thriller
by Timothy Mooney

Criteria
© 2013 by Timothy Mooney

ALL RIGHTS RESERVED

Credits:
Cover Illustration b Lee Rushton
Map Designs by Lee Rushton

ISBN 13: 978-0-9831812-3-1
ISBN 10: 0983181233
Library of Congress Control Number: 2013903389

Reviews of CRITERIA

"4 Stars" "An *engaging and brilliant* performance."   *Edmonton VueWeekly*

"A" Timothy Mooney's one-man show is ***provocative, funny, thoughtful, shocking and compelling***. Stuff like this is what the fringe is all about. See it."
Quentin Mills-Fenn, Winnipeg Uptown

"It's a sci-fi action flick, a thriller, a mystery and a road movie all boiled into a riveting one-man show… The intrigue culminates in ***an edge-of-your-seat finale*** in which the terrorist quite literally holds the fate of America in his hands."   *Cheryl Binning, Winnipeg Free Press*

"A consummate story-teller. I left the theatre with the feeling that I could listen to him tell a story about almost anything... Mr. Mooney took me somewhere I never thought I would go. *Criteria* was not without comedy either. On his journey, the terrorist enters a diner where he encounters friendly small-town locals. His shock and horror at the decadence of a society where a waitress calls everyone "honey" ***almost brought the house down...***"
Stacy Rowland, TheatreSeattle.com

"When was the last time you attended a Fringe show where, all around you, audience members were literally leaning forward in their seats, virtually mesmerized and determined not to miss a single word? It happened the other afternoon with *Criteria*, a very clever cautionary science fiction tale… ***One of the best and most original things in Fringe 2006***."*Janice Sawka, Jenny Revue*

"The world the play creates is one that any society can be reflected in... ***It approaches the arena of politics more successfully than any other show*** I've seen in this Fringe, because it does it through *metaphor* rather than through *preaching*. It's smart, it's nuanced, I loved it -- and everybody needs to see it... Don't let it slip away.   *Phillip Low, Fringe Blogger*

"Timothy Mooney's epic one-man journey into a possible future carries with it ***wonderful humor, dark speculation, and a damn great time***… It will leave you thinking about the themes for a long time."*Kale Ganann (On-line Review)*

"*Criteria **should be performed for corporate executives or at political gatherings and then discussed all night.***"
George Savage, Playwright, (On-line Review)

"A futuristic, sci-fi conspiracy thriller that ***will have you on the edge of your seat***… an adventure that will satisfy the most ardent fans of the sci-fi genre.
Ken Gordon, The Jenny Revue

"*Criteria* is a gem, and should definitely be at the top of your To-Consider List… bright and engaging… *fantastical yet so incredibly, and poignantly, timely*. Skilled storytelling and clever, intricate physicality."
Leigha Horton, On-line Review

"*One Man Apocalypse!*" "A sci-fi suspense solo show with funny moments… I enjoyed this show immensely… There's not a lot of optimism in Mooney's show (though there's plenty of apocalypse-relieving comedy), but that's the way I like it."
Courtney McLean, On-line Review

"As in good theater throughout history, Mooney has created something wonderfully uncommon from apparently prosaic materials… The language in this play is *astonishing… pulling us along, off-balance and breathless with incomprehension* … alternating between chortles and gasps. … If I laughed, it would have to have been the laugh of catastrophe: giddy with hopelessness... Mooney creates an adrenalin rush, his delivery racing along with the momentum of the train we see all too clearly... Whether you want a punch in the old ideological stomach, or just a really exciting evening of virtuoso theater, see *Criteria*."   *Richard Greene, Georgia College & State University*

"*A comic espionage sequence Woody Allen might have written*. And all for the price of a one-man show... In his confident hands, the drama unfolds at a captivating pace and the dark comedy crackles."
Fringe Review Rag, Seattle 2003

"*The action is exciting, the consequences chilling and the story telling superb*."   *Carl Gauze, Ink 19*

"Very compelling… *Hard to explain but easy to enjoy*."
Bret Fetzer, The Stranger Weekly Magazine

"He's a very good actor, with a good ear for dialogue and scenes, and he makes this ambitious notion work..."   *Roger Moore, Orlando Sentinel*

"*This isn't the idealistic 24th century predicted in Star Trek*! …I find myself laughing out loud, again and again. I'm amazed by the acting and the storytelling… I love it."   *On-line Review*

"*So much suspense I couldn't believe it was a one-man show*!"
Theatre Student (Rocky Mountain Theatre Festival)

From the Author...

Initially written in 2002, *Criteria* was only vaguely a response to what must seem like an obvious inciting event: the terror attacks of September, 2001. Certainly, without those dark events in the early days of this century, this story would not have taken the shape it now has.

But there were other things that were going on at the same time: political tangles that suggested any number of the incidents and ideas that floated in and out of this story.

I borrowed from them heavily.

I ran them through the mix-master of my mind and synthesized *Criteria*.

There was so much running through that mix-master, that I prefer not to detangle those threads, or un-mix that mixture to expose the various meats that comprise this particular sausage (to further torture a mixed metaphor). Because an awareness of those political hot potatoes may only keep the engaged reader/audience from being able to see beyond the details of issues on which they may have taken unshakeable preemptory positions.

Because, somewhat astonishingly to me, through all those that have seen *Criteria* over the years: each seems to see this play through the prism of their own political orientation: Liberals, Conservatives, Libertarians, Anarchists... have all celebrated this play, insisting that it speaks to the particulars of their own point of view.

And I hate to dissuade them of that possibility.

Sometimes, when people forget about the labels and the parties and the history that belabors multi-nuanced issues, and focus, instead, on a human being in action, with whom they may identify, they suddenly are able to "hear" a statement that they never knew that they believed... a statement which, in any other context they probably would not have agreed with. And that is the liberating gift that Science Fiction... or, more accurately, "Speculative Fiction," offers.

Just imagine, for instance, the statement that I was certain would get me in trouble: "When you make life no longer worth living, you invite terrorism." Speaking that idea aloud in September 2001 would probably have been asking for trouble... But given the character speaking it and the context of his society, we have a frame within which that notion may be contemplated and understood. Over the course of perhaps a hundred performances, no one has ever challenged that idea.

Written in the shadow of that disruptive period, I shared what was then the short story, *Criteria*, with a popular science fiction magazine, which responded enthusiastically about the material, asked for a look at any future such stories I might write, but noted that this one was not going to work for their publication.

This was still 2002-ish. Perhaps it was still too soon. Or, perhaps the short story format is just not my wheelhouse.

Not being a regular short story writer, or a regular science fiction story writer, I did not have a sense of where to go next.

I was an actor. And a director. And a writer. Sometimes I did voiceover. And I was on tour with my one-man play, *Molière Than Thou*. And all these many irons in the fire were quite enough to keep me from running down that elusive publication for a story that I wasn't entirely certain that America was ready to hear.

Assuming that nothing would ever come of it, I e-mailed copies to a few choice friends, and got back on the road.

It may have been a year or so after the actual composition that I found myself sitting at the kitchen table of a dear friend in the suburbs of Raleigh, North Carolina (*Hi, Forsyth!*), asking whether she had managed to read the story I'd sent her some several months prior. "No, I keep meaning to, but—"

"Would you mind if I read it to you?" I asked impulsively. A year past the story's born-on date, I had no actual sense of how the material "played" to the literary audience, and nothing would give me a better sense of that effectiveness, than hearing the moment-by-moment reaction of someone listening to the thing play out.

"Sure!" was her reply. I pulled out my copy of the material, we settled in at the kitchen table, and I began.

I have no idea how long that reading ran… It felt like forty-five minutes, but based on further experience with the script, I can't imagine that first reading came in under an hour-fifteen. By the time the thing was done, I was a little shocked at a number of things:

It was funny.

It was tense.

It was funny!

It was serious.

It was profound.

I came away with a new sense of how this material "played," and that may have been my first glimmer of the direction that this story would ultimately take.

Way back in the Spring of 2002, I was picking up income working as a "standardized patient:" essentially an actor who was playing the role of a patient for med students, who need to learn the notion of "bedside manner."

I often refer to standardized patient work as "the sweatshop for actors." The timing of my availability, usually at the end of the semester, combined with whatever character traits I personally exhibited, usually found me cast as the character in the final exam, which was about "Giving Bad News."

As many as twelve times a day, over the course of a week-and-a-half, I played out the scenario in which I was informed of having contracted pancreatic cancer, with an anticipated six months to live. Bad news, indeed.

Hearing this twelve times a day, over some eight days… as many as 96 times… and playing out that devastating scenario, with all of the denial, anger, and pain that ensues… can seriously damage one's mood.

And if you have any belief in psychosomatic influences, it's really not a refrain that you want running through your head over and over and over again.

In between "doctors," I would focus on less onerous thoughts: happiness and light. I was responsible for certain grading responsibilities, as I traced my way back through the encounter, filling in the little "bubbles" on the form, detailing just how effectively and accurately the doctor informed me about the nature of the disease, the survival rate, and the next steps that I must take.

[Side note: one med student, who was supposed to tell me that he was sending me for a "biopsy," actually said that he needed to send me for an "autopsy." So, yes, they do need to practice before they "practice."]

But the very first thing I needed to fill out on the chart was information to identify the students themselves. As part of the kabuki theatre that this encounter was, they would hand me their "business card," encouraging me to contact them with any questions. On this card was, in fact, the student's name and Social Security Number, which were the first two items I would fill in before proceeding to grade them on their communication skills.

And little by little, I started to notice an odd trend…

Most of the cards that I was receiving featured Social Security Numbers beginning with the number "3". Occasionally, I would get a card with a "4". Sometimes a "5," and increasingly rarely a "2" a "1" and a "0".

Nothing else.

I thought that was odd, and eventually, out of curiosity, I looked up just why the trend tilted so heavily to a given number.

I found that when this whole system was set up, back in 1936, those numbers were designed to reflect the area in which the recipient lived, at the time that they applied for their Social Security Card, like a ZIP code.

Being of a certain age, I applied for my Social Security Card at around the time that I applied for my first job. Which meant that I spent the first sixteen or so years of my life without that number following me around wherever I went. Mine is the last generation for which that will be true.

Most parents now obtain their child's Social Security Number at the same time that they obtain their birth certificate. Which means that the place of birth and the Social Security Number are irrevocably tied.

Add these circumstances to the omnipresent paranoia and homeland-security-based insecurity (airport frisks, hotel check-in forms, credit card regulations), and it struck me that we have a formula for a particular kind of disaster.

"What if...?"

What if our obsession with identity and identification led us to make more and more bad choices (like some of the disastrous choices we were currently making) placing the Social Security Number into higher prominence... ultimately manifesting itself as an actual tattoo on each citizen's palm?

What if that great "melting pot" that is the United States were to blend the racial strands of its citizenry to the point that the Social Security Number might actually outride the importance of race as a function of identity?

And what if that phenomenon that manifests itself as racism is actually a construct that human beings will create even in the absence of racial differentiation? In other words, what if we replaced "racism" with "numberism?" Because, as my lead character opines, "As long as there are distinctions between groups... groups will naturally gravitate to their own."

With these thoughts, and given my desire to distract myself between bouts of "Bad News," I started turning that speculation into a story.

Several days into the composition, I found myself writing the line that "It would be the first such diner that I had ever eaten in, actually. Little did I realize the consequences of such a stop."

It was at that point that I realized that I now had to come up with consequences to that particular stop. And what had been, up until that point, a fairly nuanced political discussion, suddenly embraced the comic soul that had been simmering beneath the surface.

When that story didn't quite find its audience at first blush, and following the aforementioned kitchen-table reading, another friend pointed out that I did have an alternative vehicle for getting my work in front of the public... I was an actor/director/producer, and I didn't need anybody's go-ahead to simply memorize the thing and perform it.

There have been major changes along the way: What began as a single linear story line has been fragmented, with jumps forward and backward in time to heighten the tension and curiosity. Whereas I initially stood still throughout the play, the addition of actual running (albeit running in place) made the performance itself into a test of stamina that every audience member seems to recall, years after having seen it.

Ultimately, *Criteria* was a successful one-man play, which I only occasionally got the opportunity to perform.

Given that my own personal "brand" revolves around the career of France's greatest playwright, Molière, and the immense catalogue of Shakespeare, it made little sense for me to push this quirky sci-fi thing on the same faculties that were hiring me to perform classical theatre.

But every once in a while, I get to do this performance… sometimes for an audience that hangs on every word. More often than not, this play actually tastes of each element of the genres that it aims at: One-Man; Comic; Sci-Fi; Thriller. People were hanging in suspense on the climax of this thing, not knowing how it was going to resolve. In spite of the fact that no one other than myself was going to enter onto the stage through the course of the performance, they were sitting forward in their chairs, almost breathless at the climax. They were laughing in all the right places. They emerged with the relief of having passed through *catharsis*.

And, they had seen their own political alignment expressed, in ways that they had perhaps thought about, but never articulated.

And now, I approach the ten-year anniversary of performing this thing. A couple of times a year, I seem to run into a *Criteria* fan… someone who saw this play eight or nine years back, who still remembers the feeling of seeing this show. Usually, what they recall is an image of me running "***throughout the entire play!***" (For the record, actual running occurs underneath about 10% of the dialogue… but this play leaves an especially kinetic impression.)

I still get to perform *Criteria* now and then, but it seems to have legs that are longer than my own. The farther that we get from the circumstances of its writing, the more people seem to appreciate it, and yet, the farther I get from the assumed age of the protagonist, or anti-hero.

So, while I may continue to perform this play from time to time (go ahead; twist my arm), it's time for somebody else to pick this thing up and run with it.

Literally.

Running, is now one of the necessary components of this play. And these days, my knees are not so good as they once were.

Break a leg!

Tim

CRITERIA

PROGRAM NOTES:

The U.S. Social Security Administration, begun back in 1936 was immediately controversial. One congressman famously intoned, "I'm warning you, that number will follow you around from birth through death." Numbers were assigned based on the location in which you applied. Numbers beginning with zero, for instance, were assigned to New England, with "ones" going to Pennsylvania/New York/New Jersey, "twos" to the southeast, and so on.

Early in the history of the Social Security Administration people would apply for their number as they began working (and had to account for their income to the Internal Revenue Service). However, as the use of social security numbers has grown, people have begun acquiring them earlier. Most people now get their numbers at about the same time that they get their birth certificate.

It struck me that the growing significance of the SSN, along with the geographical assignment of such numbers created a formula for larger, unanticipated issues.

And, yes, the proper word is, in fact, "Criterion."

ABOUT THE AUTHOR:

Timothy Mooney has adapted seventeen of Molière's plays to the stage, seen in the United States, Canada, Scotland, Italy Indonesia and India, with many of them published by Playscripts, Inc. His one-man plays, *Molière than Thou* and *Lot o' Shakespeare* are turning a new generation on to Molière and Shakespeare and his latest, *The Greatest Speech of All Time*, is opening up a new vision of history, with speeches ranging from Socrates to Martin Luther King Jr. Formerly, Tim produced fifty plays in five years as Artistic Director of the Stage Two Theatre. He taught acting at Northern Illinois University, and published his own newsletter, *The Script Review*. Tim created the TMRT Press, publishing his long-awaited acting text, *Acting at the Speed of Life* in 2011, followed by *The Big Book of Molière Monologues* in 2012. For 2013, Tim has decided to release parts of his one-man catalogue into the universe, beginning with *Criteria* and *Molière Than Thou*.

CRITERIA

Cast of Characters

THE MAN ("Adam Gardner")
THE WAITRESS ("Nancy")
THE TRUCKER ("George")

All characters are intended to be performed by the same person.

Time: 300 years (and more) into the future.

Place: Points West

CRITERIA

Optional Pre-Show Activity:

As the audience enters, an usher with a hand stamp, much as you might see at a bar or a concert, stamps the palms of the audience as they receive their programs. No explanation is given for the hand-stamping process. If any audience member objects, they are, of course, welcome to enter without having their hand stamped. They will discover, as the play goes on, that the number on their hand is the same as the number to which our protagonist repeatedly refers.

This may be a cause for concern.

Pre-Show Music:

Songs about trains.

Note:

Boldface is used to depict a speech from another time and place than the through-line of action. These speeches are usually performed in a pool of light, off to the right side of the stage.

On the Projection Screen (Stage Left):

SLIDE 1: A slide with the title of the play, perhaps with the poster illustration.

Following any pre-show announcements, THE MAN enters the stage, carrying a binder marked "EYES ONLY." He studies the audience with some combination of scorn and contemplation. Reaching for the laptop computer that runs the slide show, he triggers the first slide change, which also cues the lead-in music, "What Will the Martians Think?"

THE MAN exits, leaving the audience to study the slide as the music plays.

SLIDE 2: A historical timeline, outlining major events of US History. Several (Declaration of Independence, Civil War) are familiar to us. Others ("The Sorting," "The Incursions") are not.

Historical Timeline

Year	Event	Year	Event
1776	US Colonies submit "Declaration of Independence"	2096	Coal/Oil Supply Exhausted
1865	US Civil War	2107	US Population reaches 600 Million
1936	Social Security Administration Founded	2107 -2112	The Sorting
1989	End of "Cold War"	2112	Establishment of 6 Unions
2000	US Population reaches 287 Million	2176 -2278	The Incursions
2023	Nuclear Waste buried in Yucca Mountain	2232	Bombing of Dallas
2001 -2076	"The Terror"	2279	Three Unions: 2, 4, 5 Remain
2077	Tattoos established by Department of Homeland Security	2307	The Great Yucca Earthquake
		2341	The Shipments Begin

LIGHTS UP ON THE MAN: "Conference Room"

THE MAN's manner is tense and militarily brusque, and yet with a friendly sense of irony. He holds a binder, marked "EYES ONLY." At first he seems to be reading from it.

THE MAN

And so the war had come to this.

A man on a bridge. With the power to destroy.

The Twos had consumed the east.

The Fives owned the west.

The Fours had what lay in between.

The Zeros, the Ones, the Threes?

Slaves for the most part.

> *(Setting the binder onto a music stand in front of, and slightly to the left of, his chair, THE MAN, correcting his ill choice of words, sits down, lightens his tone slightly, no longer reading from the binder.)*

No, no, we don't call them slaves. There is no such thing as a slave these days.

But they can't own property, or any property worth owning, which amounts to just about the same thing. Just try to get into a school as a Three.

Those of us who live in what once were Zero, One, and Three lands have been rather tolerant, but let a Three show up in the east? Or a

Zero in the west? They'd have their nuts handed to them.

Of course, when you can't own property, there's not much left worth living for, save for what passes between a man and a woman. And so the lines have not died out the way that some might have hoped.

Then, there are those who insist that they should have just all been killed then and there, while we still had the chance. Perhaps the best thing would have been to get rid of them altogether, while we could still label them as a threat.

And, in a way, they were a threat, at least as far as we were concerned.

We needed space. Everybody needs space.

We were running out of numbers.

There were 99,999,999 of us. Or thereabouts.

Okay, time for a little history lesson.

287 million.

The SLIDE SHIFTS to reveal a map of the United States, headed, "The United States, circa 2000."

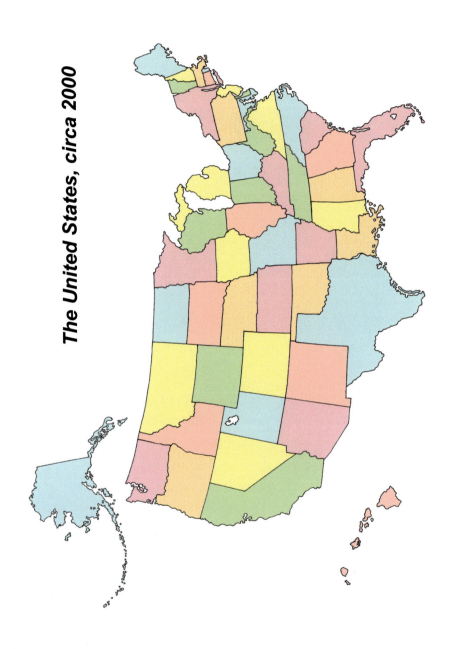

The United States, circa 2000

THE MAN (*Continuing.*)

That's the nationwide population at around the turn of the millennium. A rather manageable number, I would think. Not all that much different from what we've got now. About half. And hardly worthy of concern. Were it not for Social Security numbers.

You see, some numbers are better than others… And we were running out of the better ones.

LIGHT SHIFT: "Outdoors"

(*By the end of the light shift, THE MAN appears in a pool of light Stage Right, running as he continues to relate the story to the audience. While he is running in place, he still maneuvers in ways that anyone running across uneven terrain might: jumping over obstacles, ducking low-hanging branches, circling left or right to avoid potholes, leaning backward or forward with the tilt of the terrain. Though we wouldn't likely notice this consciously, this version of "The Man" may feel a bit younger than the character who was addressing us in the "Conference Room.")*

THE MAN (*Continuing.*)

The arrogant Fives didn't even try to keep their plans from us. After all, we had to receive the toxic stuff, so we had to know what rails it was coming in on, if only to have adequate security in place.

Their assumption was that no one could penetrate their territory far enough to bomb the caravan before it was in range of destroying all of the east along with it.

They never counted on a man with no tattoo.

We are an elite group of commandos, my brothers and I. Borrowed from the ranks of what were once Threes.

Some two dozen years ago, my mother was approached by government agents. Abandoned by my father before I was born, my mother was offered a deal. A home and some money in exchange for her boy. Her boy would be brought up under the best of circumstances on a military campus. I was trained to fight, to run and to believe in the cause. I was a success at all three.

My brothers and I had no tattoos. Brought up in seclusion, our tattoos were held in abeyance until such time as we received our

assignments. Some of us might be sent on missions to Virginia, others to California, or, Twoland and Fiveland, respectively.

(THE MAN slows to a stop.)

I look down at my hand and see my freshly minted number: 589-00-7693. Albert Gardner.

LIGHT SHIFT "Conference Room"

THE MAN *(Back in his chair, continuing)*
They had to create a criteria.

Just a single little stupid, meaningless pissant criteria.

It didn't really matter which one they chose. Any odd, idle, irrelevant stinking criteria would do it.

It was nothing more than an administrative shortcut. Some clerk, somewhere, thought that it would be easier keeping the numbers this way rather than that.

Some lousy, stinking clerk, lost in the annals of the dark ages of history.

(With a slight nod or gesture to his right hand.) Assigning Social Security numbers.

The Zeroes and Ones never had a chance.

It all goes back to the days of the Terror. Or, I should say the days when terror resurfaced as a way of life. And when it's a way of life, it really isn't terror anymore. More like… anxiety. An ongoing, underlying anxiety constantly reminding you of the fragility of it all. That it can all end tomorrow. And, of course, it always can, always could.

But you really have to go back to those days to see where Social Security numbers got so damned important. Of course, Social Security itself went out of business two hundred years ago when we broke off into six Unions. Security, huh.

But in relatively short order, at least in evolutionary or geological terms, the numbers conquered the being. You look back at films from those days and you can really see distinctions between people. Black people who are really, you know… black. White people who are entirely pale. Asians, Hispanics… you can really tell the difference! Weird.

I suppose it's not surprising that there was racial prejudice back then. After all, you knew who who was. And as long as there are distinctions between groups, groups will, naturally, gravitate to their own. That's probably worth repeating. "As long as…" ah, fuck it.

It was the tattoos, more than anything, that set things in motion. Of course, they're second… no, they're *first* nature now, but back then it was a revelation.

For a while, they had tried to make the thing work with I.D. cards, and they put all sorts of gizmos in the card for protection: holograms, fingerprints, retinal scans, DNA codes. It all got really expensive; because every time you add a gizmo at one end, you have to add more equipment at the other, and not every shopkeeper or grade school can afford their own lab just to tell whether you're somebody who has any business being there or not.

A card can be stolen. But a tattoo on your palm? Not much anybody can do to falsify that.

Of course, people tried, but when they make the penalty for altering your number the loss of your hand? *(HE bends his hand toward himself, momentarily creating the illusion that it has been cut off at the wrist.)* People tend to stick with their lot in life. Stealing an identity meant losing your identity, and without an identity, who are you? Nobody.

LIGHT SHIFT: "Outdoors"

THE MAN (*Continuing, running, once again*)
Apparently, Albert Gardner died seventeen years ago without an heir. They'll be reassigning his number any day now, but for now, I am him.

It's amazing how accustomed the authorities are to dead people showing up. No Union has a monopoly on bureaucratic mistakes, and when the checkpoints pronounce me dead, I simply sigh, roll my eyes and present my paperwork, self-evidently alive. If they need any further explanation, I speculate that some guy with a single digit's difference must have died, and some clerk killed me off with a typo.

So far, I've managed to avoid the official checkpoints. Of course, everywhere you go you have to show your tattoo (it is, after all, part of the shaking-hands ritual), but that's just a formality. They don't generally log you into a database unless you're checking into a hotel,

buying a ticket to go somewhere, or pulled into jail on a violation.

(Slowing to a stop.)

I like my hands just where they are. I plan on keeping them in place, at least for the next seventy-two hours.

After that, I'll be part of the cosmic ether. And a matter of legend.

LIGHTS SHIFT: "Conference Room"

SLIDES SHIFT to show the United States, curiously separated into six divisions, headed "The Six Unions, 2112". The man takes out a laser pointer, using it to illustrate the regions he is describing as he speaks. He does this with a mirror, strategically hidden by the script on the music stand, so that he doesn't have to turn his back on the audience.

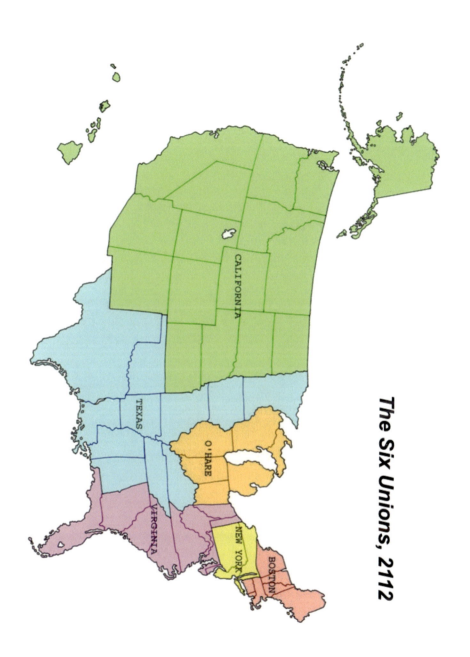

The Six Unions, 2112

THE MAN (*Continuing from his chair*)
THE SORTING. There had been a time when you could be born one place, go away to school someplace else, get a job all the way across the country somewhere. You put down fresh roots and create a home.

Except that, now, you carry that damn number around with you wherever you go. A number that had suddenly become everyone's business.

And we were running out of numbers...

> As he speaks, THE MAN "points" at the regions of the country to which he is referring, as the audience begins to attach numbers to the otherwise familiar regions in their thinking. He will repeat this process virtually every time he references a given number or regional name. When he refers to "the Zeros" he points to "BOSTON" (or the New England states); "Ones" or "NEW YORK" include the lower half of New York, most of Pennsylvania and New Jersey; "Twos" are the states south of Pennsylvania (plus eastern Ohio), marked "VIRGINIA;" "Threes" include Illinois, Wisconsin, Michigan, Indiana and western Ohio, marked "O'HARE;" "Fours" include most of the southern central states, but also run northwards to Minnesota (marked "TEXAS"), and "Fives" refers to the vast western states, all marked "CALIFORNIA."

Oh, sure, between zeros, ones, twos, threes, fours and fives, there were a potential six hundred million numbers available.

But each union had only a single hundred million to spread among its Chosen People, who were sharing from an ever-diminishing pool of resources.

The California Union has always had it the easiest of them all. A hundred million spread across more than half of the country. Having Alaska didn't hurt.

Then there were the expansion arguments. After all, a number was just a number. Why not open up the game to sixes, sevens, eights, nines? Mathematically, no issue.

But who wants to go first? Anybody want to raise their kids as the only sixes in a union of fours? Take a chance on the notion that people will be tolerant?

Or, decimals. There's lots of decimals out there. "Fractions,"they call them. Might as well hang a sign around their neck that says "bastards." Turned out to be the most successful birth control method ever. What's more, every now and again a grandparent will die, mysteriously, just before a fraction is about to be born. Each family gets a single generation to reclaim a number before it goes back into the pool. Never stays in the pool for more than a second.

Decimals are more common among the Zeros, Ones and Threes, although they're still very much frowned upon. Certain governments, notably the Twos (who have the least amount of territory but still host three indigenous populations) get a little nervous about any increase in opposing population bases. It seems that when, periodically, the decimal population goes up, so does the prison population, which is, not surprisingly, composed almost exclusively of Zeroes, Ones and Threes.

Anyway, there was that very ugly period of The Sorting during which the various numbers discovered they just couldn't live with each other. The property was too valuable, and the Outplaced were too vulnerable. Homes were torched and re-occupied. The victims would flee, generally to the state of their birth where they were safe.

When they arrived, unless they came well-funded, or had family still in the area, they would generally find the doors closed. How often did people leave behind multi-million dollar homes only to find themselves sleeping on a cot in a shelter?

It was a disruptive period of perhaps six or seven years before we were all Re-Sorted, with Zeros, Ones, Twos, Threes, Fours and Fives all in their places. And by the time that was complete, there was no need for a "United States" anymore. Because… well, we weren't "united" anymore. Of course, for a while you could still travel from one Union to another, but you really wouldn't want to go out in public.

LIGHTS SHIFT: "Outdoors"

THE MAN, (Running.)
The need for secrecy has kept me in close quarters for my entire life. There are less than fifty people who even know of my existence. The campus that we live on is perhaps three walled-in acres of a former air base now serving as a police and border patrol facility. I never even saw the rest of the facility until they brought me out to begin the mission.

Of course, you see the digitals depicting life in the outside world all the time, and many of them are still made in California (which accounts for the moral laxity of the subject matter). But just seeing regularly spaced houses, parks and even forest preserves was astounding. I felt a surge of patriotism. This was the land that I was fighting for! In the east, of course, they had no such luxury, and the digitals depicting life in the east were always gritty, angry, claustrophobic affairs. Their close proximity shortens their fuse. The other side of this is of course the great love and passion generally depicted in their relationships. It seems they have a lot of spaghetti dinners that somehow never quite wind up getting eaten.

None of this could prepare me for what I was to find out west. Smuggled across the ExKansas border, just south of Wichita, I made what distance I could during the night hours. I had studied maps and topographical surveys for the past year. I anticipated every rise and fall of the landscape. I knew what to expect... at least until the sun came up.

(Stops running.)

The concept of infinity cannot be grasped in the abstract.

I had some exposure to the concept. At night I could look above me and see the starscape, and imagine the many worlds and universes stretching away endlessly.

I had simply never applied that same principle to the land.

As the sun rose behind me, I watched the land exposing itself before me, constantly awaiting what I consciously knew would not appear: the wall at the border of the next parcel.

Instead, there were the farmhouses, set back perhaps a quarter mile from the highway. The highway itself, reaching ahead, a concrete ribbon, just as they describe it in the song, disappearing into the distance, a rippling wash of green and gold.

(Resumes running.)

I kept moving, running when I felt secure, walking when I thought someone might be watching. I had a week to make the trip and I knew that harsh terrain awaited at the far end, and so I started out by pushing myself, taking on at least a hundred miles a day.

(Winding down to a walking pace.)

Occasionally, I would come across rivers and canals, and, away

**from the highway, I would take advantage of the opportunity to strip
down and rinse out my running clothes. Trading these for my
walking costume, I would hang shorts and shirt from my belt,
allowing these to dry while continuing on at a lighter pace.**

LIGHTS SHIFT: "Conference Room"

THE MAN
(In his chair, describing the conflicts with the laser pointer.)
THE INCURSIONS: Virginia first set its sights to the south,
occupying Puerto Rico, which, for some reason had been set up as a
Five, back in the dark ages. Not only was it strategically unnecessary to
the California Union, it was probably a burden on them, as well.

From there it was on to New Jersey, which the New York Union
seemed particularly unenthused about protecting.

It became evident to everyone that Virginia's ultimate goal was the
entire Eastern Seaboard, but they had so isolated their targets that it
became virtually impossible for the Threes or Fours to come to the aid
of Pennsylvania and, later, New York, without first crossing Two
territory in Ohio.

Instead, and this is the decision that has shaped the hostility of the
past two centuries, the other Unions began to look hungrily *at each
other*. If Virginia was making a superpower of itself (which California
already was) then the Threes and the Fours would be the next target.
One or the other would need to get bigger, fast. And while the Threes
and Fours, together, might well take on all comers, and even drew up
treaties to that effect, neither felt that they could trust the other.

It was the Fours, the Texas Union, that moved first, cutting Illinois
and Indiana of the O'Hare Union off at the knees. From Iowa to
Kentucky, both territories that they already possessed, the Texas
planners drew a line and made their advance. Meanwhile, the Old
Minnesota Fours crossed the Mississippi River, cutting off the western
bend of Wisconsin.

It all sounds so simple, now, but it was perhaps a hundred years of
incursion, treaty, occupation, treaty, violation, treaty, and further
incursion. Every time that the Texans seemed satisfied, they would find
another territory to occupy, be it the upper peninsula of Michigan, or
Western Ohio. Every ten years or so, they would grasp for another ten
percent of what remained, until the central hub of O'Hare was the last

piece to fall.

(Lowering the laser pointer.)

Need I point out that blood spilled? Terror was the weapon of choice, and these proud northerners were not eager for slavery. The mistake that every occupying force seems to make is in creating a devalued life for the natives. When you make life no longer worth living, you invite terrorism. Be it bombers, snipers, or kidnappers: the sharper the decline in the quality of life, the greater the increase in guerilla activity.

No one knows just how the bombers got through to Dallas, but the Cohen brothers were whispered heroes throughout the occupied O'Hare Territories for the better part of a decade.

(Resuming pointing out geographical issues.)

Over the years there were minor reckonings to be made, and it was the former "panhandle" states that seemed to fare the worst. Oklahoma reached too far into perceived California territory, as did western Texas. Western Florida had to be amputated from its former peninsula, and the odd serrated edge created by Tennessee and Kentucky's perceived intrusion into Virginia territory had to be adjusted.

Up in the Northeast, many of the zeroes fled into Canada, and the Canadians took them… They need their slaves too.

LIGHTS SHIFT: "Outdoors"

THE MAN *(Running)*
Food, a canteen, one change of clothes, I.D. cards, the components of a tiny device, and sunblock. I was traveling light.

There was no way of carrying sufficient food for the trip. With the energy I would be expending, I would need at least thirty to forty pounds of nutrition to sustain me, but such a load would make the running, already a challenge, virtually impossible. It was not the weight, so much as the bulk.

For these first few days, however, I stuck to the menu provided, consuming most of the stores that I was carrying. The objective was to get far from the border, and the presumably more suspicious homesteaders, before allowing myself the convenience and the pleasure of a public diner.

It would be the first such diner that I had ever eaten in, personally. Little did I realize the consequences of such a stop.

(Slowing to a stop.)

I had left Kansas behind, and was entering the town of Lamar. My running clothes were washed, dried and packed away. My pack was fifteen pounds lighter than when I'd started. Fortunately, well-trimmed beards and closely-cropped hair were in fashion, so I didn't have to carry extra toiletries for their upkeep.

I was, however, noting the impact that the running was having on my skin. The sunblock was sweating off quickly after application, and the portions left exposed were turning a deeper red.

The concern was that sunburn was clearly NOT the style of choice. Anyone who cared to notice would know that I had been outside without protection.

Well, so be it. I have to eat. And for once I am in a town, and I feel safe.

LIGHTS SHIFT: "Conference Room"

SLIDES SHIFT, revealing a third map featuring a United States with three divisions. ("The Three Unions, 2279-Present")

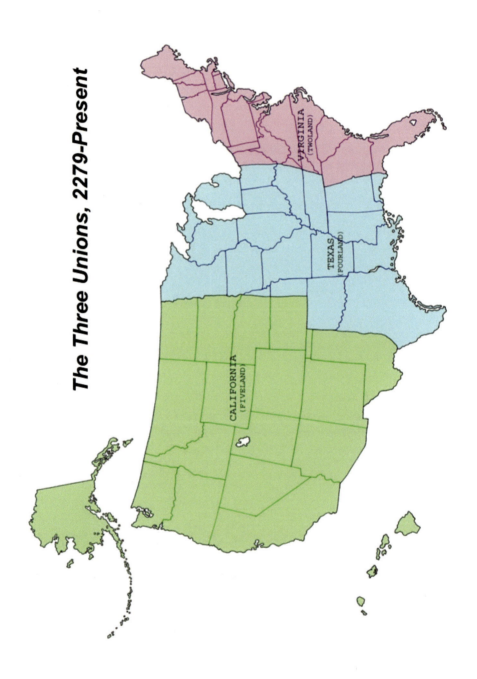

The Three Unions, 2279-Present

VIRGINIA
(TWOLAND)

TEXAS
(FOURLAND)

CALIFORNIA
(FIVELAND)

THE MAN (*Reappearing in his chair.*)
So. Three unions, each perhaps half the width of the union to its immediate west, with more or less smooth edges.

And now, the nuclear waste was coming back.

Somebody thought they had sealed it up for good a few centuries back. Well, there was that little fault line not far from Yucca Mountain. (*Using the laser to indicate a spot in Nevada.*) The containers themselves were unbroken, but the vault had cracked and now all bets were off. It gave the Fives the opportunity to reverse what they had always considered to be a rather egregious decision. Perhaps when we were all one United States it made sense to have a single storage facility. All your eggs in one basket, as it were.

But Pandora's Box was open, and the nukes were going home.

There was nothing that the Twos or Fours could do about it. The wind prevails out of the west. An attack from the east would create a spill which would send the fumes over Texas and Virginia. The best that they could hope would be to graciously receive the toxic stuff, delicately redirecting it to storage facilities of their own.

Of course nothing much gets shipped anywhere these days. Having run out of coal and oil long ago, we're now left with solar, wind and nuclear. People have learned to work from home, or within a mile or two of where they live. The Zeros, Ones and Threes, of course, live in the homes of their masters, the Twos, the Fours and Fives. If something has to be shipped anywhere, it's usually food.

This, of course, gives the California Union yet another advantage: more sun. Not only do they have nearly twice the territory of the other unions put together, they get their energy, largely, for free.

(*Holding back his evident anger.*)

They are a lazy, self-serving, self-indulgent race. They have grown soft, negligent, self-assured. Left to their own devices, they will continue to prosper, even as their souls decline in neglect. They will maintain their 2,000 square-foot homes with no conquered peoples to care for. While their population holds steady, at just over a hundred million, our two great unions provide for the refugees of the Zero Wars, the One Wars and the Three Wars. And now, they ship to us the stinking refuse of the nuclear neglect of a bygone era. They go back on their previous commitments. Given their economic situation, they will one day turn their attention east and *roll right over us.*

They must go.

BLACKOUT.

(THE MAN clears the music stand out of the way, upstage.)
THE WAITRESS *(In BLACKOUT.)*
"Hi, Honey, have a seat, I'll be right with you."

LIGHTS UP: "The Diner"

THE MAN

The waitress' greeting was a bit startling. I don't suppose I had been called "Honey" before, ever. And certainly she had never seen me before. In fact, she had barely looked up. This was going to take some getting used to.

(Looking back toward his chair, which he now treats as the seat of the booth in the diner.) I checked out the array of seating options, and a distant booth along the window seemed both comfortable and secure, far enough away from the door, and yet with a view of the street. A door next to the booth seemed to lead back to a kitchen area, which would imply an alternate escape route, should an emergency arise. Of course the notion of an emergency was impossible. If I was found out, there would be no escape. My only choice would be to quickly assemble the device *(Unconsciously reaching toward his belt and the shoulder strap of his pack, reminding himself of the well-practiced assembly of the two halves.)* and destroy any evidence of my existence. That, of course, would mean failure, and there was no room for failure in the face of the Fives and their bloated, godless existence.

(As he sits down, his head is momentarily turned towards the floor as he speaks, again, in the voice of "THE WAITRESS.") "What'll you have, Honey? Cup of coffee?"

THE MAN *(Resuming in his own voice.)*
(Looking up.) "Yes... please... Honey."

(THE MAN begins to alternate quickly and freely between three distinct voices: his own voice as the narrator, that of THE WAITRESS, and a slightly younger, more naïve voice of himself, caught in the glare of the Waitress' headlights, as it were. He may adjust his focus upwards, as if looking up to a standing Waitress, or downwards, as though the Waitress

20

were looking down at a sitting man.)

I added that last as an afterthought. I didn't want to seem cold or unacquainted with local custom. But it clearly drew her attention. She glanced back at me with a curious smile.

I chastised myself for my slip.

When the waitress returned, she seemed to see me for the first time, her mouth opening wide.

"Oh, Honey, you been outside? Look at that neck!"

"Oh, it's... nothing. Just a little outdoor work."

"Well, Darlin', put on the sunblock. That's a red just this side of skin cancer. We can't have that!"

"Oh, yeah, I keep forgetting to put it on... It sweats off and I need to keep reapplying it."

"Look you need some aloe or something fer that. I got some up at the front counter."

"No really, that's –"

"Cream 'r sugar with your coffee?"

"You got sugar?"

I caught myself the moment it had slipped out of my mouth. Damn that woman. She had made me forget where I was!

"Course we got sugar, Sugar. Where you been?"

And she was gone again.

Fool! I had tasted sugar once or twice in my life: holiday celebrations. I knew that sugar was plentiful in Fiveland, as they received it directly from Hawaii. Even the Twos had sugar from Florida and Puerto Rico! But the Texas Union had no such supply. My surprise at their supply would immediately reveal me as an outsider. Between sunburn and sugar, I might as well have walked in announcing myself as a spy.

"Here you go, Honey. You know what you want yet?"

Ah. The menu! Of course! You *order* things.

"Not... not just yet."

"Just gimme a holler."

I am such a fool.

(*HE pantomimes the opening of a sugar packet, which he empties and stirs into the coffee*) I contemplated leaving now, making the remainder of the trip on an empty stomach. Used sparingly, I could stretch the provisions for another couple of days. I would need water, but I was finding water fairly regularly. Yes. I could do it. (*Sipping the coffee, noticeably startled by how good it tastes.*)

But to leave now would be to draw even more attention to myself. My mistakes would be amplified. "He didn't even eat!" the waitress would report. "Honey came in here, not knowing about sugar, not knowing about the menu. Darlin' was beet red from the sun. He's clearly not one of us." And thus would the authorities be alerted.

No, I had to see it through.

A bell rang as the door opened.

THE WAITRESS
"Sit anywhere, Honey."

THE MAN
Another Honey. Were they all "Honeys" to her? Clearly this was a frivolous, degenerate society. The sleazy hostess was the love plaything to every passer-by who came through her stop.

The broad-shouldered trucker headed back my way. I watched, horrified, as rather than staking out his position at the opposite end of the diner, he invaded my own personal space. He was going to take the table right next to mine. Not the next booth, which at least would leave him facing in the opposite direction, but the table to my immediate left, where I would remain subject to his scanning gaze.

He smiled… the loathsome smile of bloated satisfaction.

THE TRUCKER
(*Speaking, now, in a fourth voice: a comfortable western drawl.*)
"Howdy."

THE MAN
"How… er, hi!" I replied. Why had no-one taught me the proper reply to a howdy?!

Unfazed, the trucker continued to sit down, still smiling the self-satisfied smile of the elite.

(THE TRUCKER's posture is relaxed, looking to the right toward the MAN, while THE MAN's position is more forced, glancing left toward THE TRUCKER... When THE WAITRESS returns, she will place herself between THE MAN, to her right, and THE TRUCKER, to her left. Aside from obvious tone-of-voice/character clues, we will know who is speaking, often, by the direction they are looking, even though THE MAN never leaves his chair.)

"Pretty bright day out there today, eh? I see you got some sun."

Damn! Was I that obvious? Why not just wear a nametag that says 'Mad Bomber?'

"Ye-p," I squeezed out, helplessly.

"Here you go, Honey, I knew I had some aloe up front."

The waitress again! Still calling me honey! Even after her latest "honey" had arrived. Had she no shame?

"Thanks. What do I owe you?"

"Oh, Darlin', don't you worry about it. You just cover up, wouldja? Hurts me just to look at you."

That was an insult, I supposed. But I managed a smile, even as I uncapped the tube.

"Y'know what you want yet?"

Ah! How long would this torture go on! Again, I had neglected to look at the menu...! "Not just yet."

"You take your time... Honey, you know what you want?" She had turned to the trucker.

"Gimme the Denver omelet, Sweetheart."

Would they never stop with their endearments!?

"You got it, Babe. Darlin, don't forget to do your ears. Here, give me that."

She took the tube back out of my hands.

And proceeded to apply the stuff to my ears!

(With his head leaning first toward one shoulder, and then to the other.) Is this how the food industry was run in this degenerate society? Do food handlers routinely massage the ears of their clientele before fetching

their dishes? Such brazen audacity!

Although, I have to admit that it felt fairly good.

"There. Now your neck. Oh, Honey, this is gonna peel! What you been wearing outside?"

Fortunately, that seemed to be a rhetorical question.

"There, now I'm going to trust you to do your hands… and your arms, from the looks of it. Honey, would you keep an eye on this one? He seems to need looking after."

"You got it, Doll."

There seemed to be no end to their array of syrupy nick-names!

"Lemme get that order in for you," she said, heading for the cook's window.

"You know, I'll have the Denver omelet, too," I spoke up, not wanting to order anything but the established entree.

"Good choice, Honey. Comin' right up."

I had barely caught my breath before…

"So where you headin?"

The trucker was just as intrusive as the waitress! If he started touching my ears, I was going to run!

"Just working my way out to Durango. Got a job lined up there, cutting and planting some trees." At least I had my cover story straight. And my Five accent was flawless.

"A job out in Durango? Not bad. Where you comin from?"

"Wichita."

"That's quite a move. You walk that whole way?"

"Yeah. It's a nice walk."

"Nice! You done covered three hundred of the boringest, most interminablest miles in the known universe. Why didn't you hitch?"

"Hitch?"

"Sure. Folks'd be happy to give you a ride."

Just how decadent *was this society*?! What kind of fools would willingly open their vehicle to attack?

"I'm enjoying the walking."

"Well, you're a better man than I, that's all I can say. Look, the least you can do is let me give you a lift as far as Alamosa."

"Oh, no, I couldn't…"

"I'm heading that way anyway. I turn south to take a load of grain to Santa Fe, but I got a passenger seat standing empty."

"No, really, I'm enjoying the walk."

"I can't imagine anybody enjoying that walk."

"No, it's great."

"Buddy, I don't know what your definition of 'great' is, but it sure don't match up with anybody else I know from around here."

I smiled, pretending to be mildly amused and hoping he would drop the conversation. Again, I had found myself caught out, not fitting in. And even this guy was tossing endearments my way.

"Omelets should be right up. You taking care of him, Sugar?"

"Trying to, Doll. He's a stubborn one though."

"I can see that. Has he at least done his arms yet?"

"Not only has he *not* done his arms, he's refused my offer of a ride twice, now."

"Oh, Darlin, am I gonna have to take you on myself?"

"No, Ma'am," I spoke up, not really knowing what "taking me on" might mean.

"Well, then you're gonna have to show me that you're capable of takin care of yourself then. Here you are, burnt to a crisp, and this nice fella is offering to take you in outta the sun for a while. And, by the way, who are you calling Ma'am?"

"I'm sorry?"

"Last fella in here called me Ma'am got a cup of hot coffee in his lap."

"I'm sorry… Honey?"

"That's more like it. Now you take that ride from this nice fella and we'll hear no more about it."

"Yes, Ma-…um, Sugar."

She smiled. "Now you're gettin the idea, Sweetheart."

I was drowning in treacle. Where was that food?

"You gotta get used to Nancy. Once she gets her mind made, she don't listen to no excuses."

She had a name! "You come here often, then?" Somehow I had to get the focus back off of myself.

"Oh, sure, I come through here twice a week. Once heading west, and then again on my way back east. Never fail to drop in to see Nancy along the way."

"Here you go fellas." Nancy was back with two plates of Denver omelets. At last, I could fill my mouth and stop giving myself away.

"I still haven't seen you do those arms, yet, Doll."

"Oh, I'll get them," I said between forkfuls.

"Honey, slow down! You're going to choke yourself."

I looked up to notice that the trucker had yet to take his first bite. These people had *dining etiquette* issues! When would I stop undermining my position?

Life on the campus was nothing like this. There was no menu, nor any wait for the food. Sixteen men ate sixteen identical meals in eight minutes. With no conversations… and no lotions.

"All right, Honey, now roll up them sleeves."

"Oh, that's all right. I'll get them."

"You gonna give me trouble, Sugar?"

"N–…no."

"Alright then, roll up them sleeves. You go ahead and eat. I'll take care of you."

I rolled them up, and there were the gasps of mock horror from the hostess. Protestations and warnings of skin cancer.

"How's them legs, Honey? You got them covered?"

"Oh yeah, they're fine."

"You gonna make me take them trousers down to find out?"

"No, really, they're fine."

"I'll wait."

I tried ignoring her.

"You got undies on under those?"

"Of course I've got un-…dies."

"All right, then, lose the pants."

"Is this how you treat your customers around here?"

"Only the ones flirting with skin cancer, and you seem to be the only one I've seen in some fifteen years, here."

"You mind if I eat… first… Honey?"

"Oh, sure, Sugar. Eat up. But I'm not lettin' you out that door 'til I check them legs. George?"

"Yeah, doll?"

"You be my enforcer? He's not going anywhere, right?"

"You got it, doll."

I was prisoner to their perverted scheme! What sort of lazy, soft-skinned, self-indulgent, bourgeois *slackers* were these Fives?

(THE MAN stands, beginning to unhook his belt.)

I was not to escape without losing my trousers and subjecting myself to yet another chorus of her indulgences. And after that, there was simply no way of refusing the ride.

LIGHTS SHIFT: "Outdoors"

THE MAN
(Reappearing in his light, jogging easily.)
Yes, there will be a time during which the land will be uninhabitable. Perhaps twenty, fifty years, the land will recover and absorb. And then it will be ready for us again. The Fours will inherit the West. There may be some Threes who will run the gauntlet of the Mississippi and the nuclear winter in order to claim homes in the west, before it is ready. And, frankly, some Fives will survive. The wind projections are for a rare northeaster, but none of the simulations that we've run so far have forecast a contamination of the former Five strongholds of Washington or Oregon.

LIGHTS SHIFT "The Diner."

THE MAN

(Returning to the "Diner," completing the task of lowering his trousers.)
I was more than a little discomfited by the attentions of the waitress, who could not resist making embarrassing and inappropriate jokes about my "package."

I imagine you snickering at what I can only refer to as "culture shock." My experience with women had been limited... virtually non-existent, were it not for the prostitutes that the government occasionally brought in to satiate our less palatable desires. With them, however, there had been no conversations. They were objects for use, not subjects capable of by-play.

We wore gloves with the prostitutes. None could know that there were tattooless government agents waiting to infiltrate enemy territory.

And here was this woman, teasing, talking, flirting, touching, *stooping* before me with her bosoms practically exposed. The trucker shrugging, smirking, pretending to block the exit while she worked on me. I was captive to their comic torment.

> *(THE MAN draws his pants back up, zips and buckles, as THE WAITRESS speaks.)*

"Goodbye, Darlin. Stop in again to see me on your way back. Maybe you won't be in such a hurry, then, and I can give you a little lotion where it counts."

I struggled to laugh off her pathetic flirtation. And yet, I hate to admit it, but there was a part of me that wanted to not have to rush off quite so quickly. And I regretted that there would, in fact, be no "way back" from my mission.

Of course, I immediately shamed myself for dangerous thinking. Certainly, I needed to do what I could in order to fit in among these self-absorbed dilettantes, and my desire to stay there and trade barbs with this woman was simply an extension of the role I was playing. I was "in character," as it were, and as long as I was in character, of course I would enjoy her flirtation, her attention, her... handiwork. But the mission lay before me, and she... lay behind me.

I prayed that "George" would not be so chatty in the truck as he was in the restaurant.

> *(THE MAN "exits" the diner, pivots, and returns, now treating the same chair as if it were the passenger seat in the truck.)*

LIGHTS DIP AND RAISE TO "Vast Outdoors" Setting

(Sitting, once again. THE TRUCKER, in the driver's seat, speaks toward his right, while THE MAN, in the passenger seat, speaks left.)

"That all you got with you?" he said as I dropped my pack into the front seat.

"Traveling light," I responded, hoping he wouldn't give it another thought.

"Hope you got a change of clothes waiting for you at the other end."

(THE MAN "watches" the landscape passing to the right and left of the truck.)

The wide-open highway was even more impressive at forty miles an hour. I stared out at the passing landscape, quietly thrilled at the walking distance he was saving me. As long as I managed to avoid giving myself away, I would cut two days of walking off of my trip, enabling me to stroll at a leisurely pace into Durango.

The land had begun to rise and fall in rolling hills, and while I knew, intellectually, what was coming, there was no intellectual way of preparing for the moment.

Nothing that could prepare anyone for that moment.

(Reflexively clutching for air.) I let out a gasp.

"First time you seen mountains, boy? Hoo-man! And you thought Kansas was pretty!"

"Well, you know, I've seen the digitals..."

"Never really quite the same thing. Where you been all these years?"

"Oh, you know, taking care of my family. My mother's been ill."

"You leave her at home all alone?"

"Oh, no, she... she died, actually. Couple months back. I just stuck around long enough to set her affairs in order."

"Sorry to hear that, son. Nobody else at home to keep you around? Wife, kids?"

"Oh, no. I never... you know, fell in much with the women."

"Handsome fella like you? You're not gay, are you?"

"No!"

"Allright! No need to get freaky on me. Just checkin."

I had forgotten about the decadent permissiveness that had overtaken this society. Sex and sexuality were considered legitimate topics for conversation. I was going to have to suspend my reflexive moral indignance if I wanted to protect my identity.

"Sorry, just got a little excited, there."

"Cause, if you're not, then you really should think about droppin back in on Nancy, there. She seemed interested, and a woman like that should have a fella around to take care of her."

"Oh, I doubt that I'd be very good for her. I'm sort of a nomad."

"Well, for a nomad, you sure don't seem to get out much."

"What do you mean?"

"What, the sunburn, the walking, the attitude. You don't strike me as one who's traveled very much… up till now."

"I meant more… socially. A social nomad."

"Course you do."

We drew closer and the mountains loomed higher, until we were on the mountains themselves, climbing, and weaving. I struggled to restrain my natural expressions of awe.

"'Sallright, son. Let it out. They're mountains. You should be amazed."

"Wow!"

"Damn right, wow. That's why I love this job so much."

"And I thought that Kansas…"

"Yeah, well that's where you're a little weird. Kansas is just Kansas. But these? These is mountains! Ain't nothing more beautiful in the whole wide world."

"Incredible!"

"Damn straight."

"Amazing!"

"That's it, Son, let it out."

"Whee-hoo!"

> *(Startling himself by this sudden, shocking release of emotion.)*

I relaxed! For the first time since crossing the border. Since the first time I could remember, really.

I reminded myself of the incredible unfairness of the situation: Thousands of square miles of beautiful space absolutely unused, abandoned, forsaken. And these blithe, uncaring, unwitting burghers oversaw the waste of the most precious resource imaginable. Could the army of Fours ever possibly take this land for granted?

Two exhilarating hours later, we were in Alamosa, where George's road turned south, and mine continued west.

> *(Stepping out of "the truck," grabbing, putting on and adjusting the invisible-to-us pack on his shoulders.)*

I got out, reminding myself to express an enthusiasm for the job I was anticipating, as well as a gratitude for the ride. I wondered what code word I might be able to use to reassure George that he had spent his hours in the company of a brethren.

"Thanks... Bud."

"My pleasure, Albert. Just stay out of the sun, eh? And knock 'em dead on your new job!"

"You got it."

"See you back at Nancy's at the end of planting season."

"Will do."

"And keep that package in your pants!"

And he was gone. Yes, the dialogue was lame. But I was playing not-to-lose, and a misstep here could send George directly to the authorities.

> *(THE MAN looks out over the audience.)*

I turned west, and allowed the vast majesty of the surroundings to set in.

Mountains. Real mountains. It was distracting. Diverting.

I spun in a circle. Three hundred sixty degrees of mountains.

And then I remembered: the loathsome, lazy Fives.

Who could never possibly deserve this.

Westward I turned, and onward I walked.

> (THE MAN walks, changing posture and his style of walking with each description of a new landscape or discovery.)

Three beautiful days. Walking the highway. Cutting across corners, down steep hillsides, along narrow ravines. Stumbling across rivers and even waterfalls.

Staying away from diners.

I had stepped into wonderland. Every two minutes I covered more territory than I had crossed in twenty-four years of living.

Which I was now loathe to call living.

This would make a magnificent home for the Fours. And the Threes.

(Stopping short.) I wondered, for a moment, which one I was. I was born to a woman who was a Three, brought up by the Fours. And looking down at my hand?

Another answer stared me in the face.

I was another of the loathsome, lazy Fives.

Or, at least, that was my character. I couldn't wait to vaporize that offending number from my hand.

(Walking again.) This self-indulgent Five spent three self-indulgent days, wandering the woods and hills. Gradually working his way to Durango.

Everything was falling into place, just as it should.

Everything.

I slept uneasy, the night before. I finished off the last of my provisions, filled my canteen with water, and made my way to the final destination. By mid-afternoon, I had come across the railroad tracks, following them for perhaps ten miles. I kept a quarter mile between myself and the railway, in case an advance team should come through, scouting the tracks.

I was hungry… A Denver omelet would have gone over very well right about now.

Of course, the hunger wouldn't bother me for very much longer.

(Stopping.) And there, in the distance, just where they said it would be. The overpass.

A logging road crossed over the train tracks, which were cut into the hillside. *("Climbing.")* With two hours to spare, I climbed the hill, taking in the landscape. The higher I climbed, the farther that I could follow the tracks with my eyes, which disappeared around the bend of a nearby hill, reappearing around subsequent hills, stretching seven, ten miles into the distance. *(Stopping at the top of the "hill.")* A train traveling fifteen to twenty miles an hour would give me at least a half an hour to get back down the hill and get into place.

LIGHTS SHIFT: the narrower "Outdoors" Setting

THE MAN
(Appearing for the first time in this isolated space NOT running.)
I'm to hit the train in Colorado, just north of a spot once known as "Four Corners," where four of the former states once shared a common point. The plume will quickly despoil all four states. From there, we are dependent upon the wind, and the way that it looks today, it should be on course to destroy Las Vegas and Los Angeles. With any luck, we'll get San Francisco in the process. I can't imagine anyone who will shed a tear for any of the above.

Shame about Mexico, though.

LIGHTS SHIFT: "Vast Outdoors"

And so, I looked. I looked, knowing that I would be the last man to look. The last man to see *this* landscape from *this* perspective.

These Fives, the bloated, God-forsaken Fives.

They didn't know what they had.

The texture, the detail.

The incredible… bumpiness of it all.

I come from a world of smooth, antiseptic walls and tiny, manicured lawns. Where action is responding to an order. Where exercise is interacting with a machine. Where love… is an act of employment.

It is *not* a world of frivolity. Of base self-indulgence. Of neglectful, irresponsible banter. Of the invasion of personal space.

Of… bumpiness.

The incredible bumpiness. The cracks and crevices, each hiding a new wonder, each bursting with life: vegetation, insects, small mammals and birds. A single acre of this land would be *treasured* in Fourland. But these Fives? Where were they? I hadn't seen a single one of them all day long! So abundant was their gift that they could afford to neglect it, ignore it. They looked at this landscape and were as unmoved as though they were staring at the neatly manicured lawn that surrounded my home!

My former home.

In my mind's eye, I couldn't recreate my home.

It was as natural to me as was my own face in the mirror.

And then I started wondering about my face.

I knew that the sun had done its work on my face. My beard had grown out to seven-days' length. I wondered if anyone back at the base would even recognize me now.

I found myself staring at my hand.

No, this would not identify me... as me.

Which begged the question.

Who was I?

I was a nameless man, in the guise of Albert Gardner, who had a date with a train, which was now appearing! In the distance! Rounding a bend in the hill, ten miles away, sending a plume of steam a hundred feet into the air.

A steam engine. Solar panels fed a battery, which heated a coil and boiled the water. Glorious steam shot up into the air, dissipated, cooled, and fell to the ground.

My hand slipped to my belt. There, one half of a tiny nuclear device sat in the clasp of my belt, looking like nothing more than a decorative orb.

The other hand drifted to the shoulder strap of my pack. Another orb awaited a reunion with its brother.

(*Taking a few steps...*) And there I descended. One final look to the train, counting the many, slow-moving cars. Eighty... seven cars stretched over half a mile. There would be no timing issues. With the train travelling at a cautious ten miles an hour, it would take at least three minutes to pass a stationary point. At any point during those three minutes, I could hurl the orb, dive with the orb, drop the orb, or simply set the orb to explode, running back into the hills to meet my fate from a distance.

Either way, the explosion would kill me. There was no escaping that. It would vaporize everything within five miles of ground zero. The ensuing cloud would poison everything within a hundred miles, and the prevailing wind will carry that poison along a widening swath for perhaps a thousand miles or more.

The prevailing wind.

Had it shifted?

No, it couldn't have. I had rounded a bend in a hill, and the wind from the northeast had temporarily seemed to shift into the northwest. It was nearly seventeen hundred hours, and the sun slanted well into the west.

Just where the wind was.

No, it's impossible! It was the terrain! The hill to the east was blocking the prevailing breeze.

All I have to do is to continue descending. As I step out onto the bridge, the wind will resume its natural direction.

Of course, a strong wind from the west would kill the mission. There was no interest in sending radioactive clouds back in the direction of Fourland, some six hundred miles behind me now. But whatever it was, this was not a strong wind. Even if it was heading in the wrong direction – *which it simply could not be!* – this wind would not carry the plume over my homeland.

My former homeland.

I am a man without a homeland, now. My future is as a vapor, giving greater glory and renewed life to the place of my birth. And, my people!

Somehow every reassurance seems to take my thinking down an unexpected, uncomfortable path.

I was thinking too much! I am a man of action! This is the moment that I have awaited, and at last, I step out onto the bridge.

The act is virtually complete already. I don't even need to await the arrival of the train. It is in range, and even at this distance, the explosion will vaporize the train and all of its contents, level the surrounding mountains and send the cleansing vapor on its way.

The cleansing vapor.

I watch the steam from the train rise up into the air. It shoots upwards before turning west, misting harmlessly to the ground.

It… turns… *west!* Which means that the wind *is* coming out of the east! The act will have its intended result! I am the hero.

> *(Reaching for his belt and his shoulder strap, he pantomimes grasping two halves of a device which he somehow screws and latches into a functional whole. He continues to handle it, for most of the remaining action.)*

I assemble the device, still watching the train, watching the vapor rise, and turn west.

Is it *turning* west? Or is the motion of the vapor an illusion due to the eastward motion of the train? Of course the steam would never rise and blow in *front* of the train; it would always trail behind! Unless the speed of the wind somehow outstrips the speed of the train.

And still the train continues to approach!

If I explode the thing now, then at least the initial thrust of the explosion will be to push the poison backwards! Westward! Against the incoming motion of the train. At least until it exhausts its momentum and continues on in whatever new direction the wind may dictate.

But I will need to act now!

The train continues to approach… I continue to assess the wind.

I imagine the wind only slightly turned, with a light breeze out of the west. To the west, the poison will carry only somewhat, perhaps as far as Las Vegas, if we are lucky. To the east it will drift more confidently, beyond the line of mountains, through Colorado and into Kansas. Surely it will stop before reaching Fourland.

Can I be sure? Certainly the damage done will be minimal at this distance. A small price to pay. But for what? This destruction might not even reach any of the major population centers. It would do most of its damage in the local towns: Durango, Santa Fe, Alamosa… even that little town with the diner. What was it? Lamar.

(Suddenly disgusted.)

The little town with the diner. And the waitress. The bloated, intrusive, bourgeois, self-satisfied, *violating* waitress with her "Honeys" and her "Sugars"!

(THE MAN's speech picks up in pace and urgency.)

The train is upon me. Fifty yards and closing. Surely I am simply raving! I am choosing to imagine the wind blowing whatever direction I want it to go. It has not changed. It will prevail! I will prevail! I will *not* anticipate, but will let the train plunge forward, striking my blow for the Fatherland in the exact middle of the train where the destruction will be the greatest!

The engine passes below me, bathing me in a burst of steam. I'm high enough above it for safety.

Ha! "Safety!" A minute before death, and I'm still worried about scalding! Such a joke! I'll have a great laugh over that when…

There is no when. None but I will ever laugh at that joke. I count the cars as they pass. *Ten cars have already slipped by.*

The train is eighty-seven cars long. Half of that would be…

Forty-three. Or forty-four.

Well, which will I hit? The forty-third or forty-fourth car?

Surely it makes no difference! The middle is the middle! One car one direction or the other cannot possibly make a difference of more than a mile's worth of destruction one way or the other! But which way? Hitting the forty-third car might be the difference between poisoning Lamar or not.

"Lamar?" Again!

Twenty cars. Amazing how ill-protected the train is! Here is their greatest toxic risk, passing through the most beautiful land imaginable, and these Fives, these bloated, God-forsaken *bastards* leave it to chug indolently through, never noticing the armed terrorist on the bridge!

Thirty cars.

I will cast the thing into the **space** between car number forty-three and forty-four! That is the midpoint!

If I were a Five, I would certainly be protecting the train better than this. I would post armed guards on every car, ready to take out terrorists such as myself! I would place checkpoints along the train tracks in order to arrest anyone suspicious! I would send a **decoy train** along the passage **first**, drawing the *fire* of any such terrorist, before allowing the real train to come along behind!

(HE *thinks.*) No! It's impossible! These are the Fives! The bloated, self-indulgent Fives! They simply don't have the sense!

Forty cars.

(Racing.)

That's the problem with them! They don't think like I do! They would never send an empty train…!

Forty-one.

Was it obvious? Should I have realized before? If I am exploding an empty train, just what impact might my death have?

Forty-two.

My death? What does my death matter? Look at the land! There is only the land and my hand, ready to…

Forty three! The space between the cars! It's now or… or…!

> *(Rearing up to hurl the device, THE MAN "bobbles" it upwards and "catches" it, essentially stopping it from falling to the train, below.)*

The forty-fourth car.

It has to be a fake train! This cannot be it. Exploding this train will be no victory for the fatherland! All I would succeed in doing is to despoil thousands of square miles of land. And what would that do?

Fifty cars.

The real train is perhaps ten miles behind. Or maybe it's a hundred miles behind! But this could not be it! Would not be it! I would not *let* this train be it!

Quick, answer the question! What would that do? *If* a nuclear device goes off in the wilderness, all that it manages to do is… to alert the Fives of the ill-intent of a *nuclear power.* A nuclear power which must be the Fours! Who else could have penetrated this far? Who else waits to claim Fiveland?

Its cities and its missiles still intact, the Fives retaliate.

Sixty cars.

They retaliate! And the missile that they send can not *not* find its target! There is no Four target that is not populated! Nine days out of ten the wind prevails out of the west. Death and misery follow!

How could my masters not have realized this? Why did they not alert me as to what I might find? They raised me as a killing machine, taught me enough to know to create the greatest destruction possible, but they never taught me how to think.

Well, I am thinking now!

Seventy cars.

Which is the greater disaster? Exploding the train, or a thinking killer? *Thought* is the enemy. I can hear the voice of my master in the back of my head. "You are not trained to *think*. *You* are to *do*. You must do and do *now*! Now! *Now, now, now!*"

(Reaching one leg, and then the other over an invisible railing, a railing which he continues to grasp behind his back.) I climb over the railing of the bridge, holding on from the opposite side.

Eighty cars.

I tuck the device in my belt. All I have to do is simply drop onto the top of one of the cars. It doesn't matter if it's car number one or car eighty-seven! The destruction will be the same.

Eighty-five.

No time for thought now, this is the time for action! And that is what I have been brought up to believe in. The power of personal action! The responsibility of the individual! And the glory of the Fours!

(Miming a shift into slow motion.) I begin to fall! ...my hands letting... go... of... the... rail...!

And... *(Back in "real time.")* grasping the rail once again!

The hand that released from the rail has a number on it.

589-00-7693.

My master's voice is silent in my head.

I have no more master anymore.

I am Albert Gardner.

It is no act of mercy.

The Fives are still the Fives: Western scum... bloated, self-indulgent, self-serving, self-righteous... Self! Self! Self!

And now… I am one of them!

And while I have been trained to die, to hate, and to fulfill on my mission at all costs, I somehow could not follow through, if it meant that I would be deprived of yet another day in these surroundings.

I know! It's ridiculous! I was prepared to spend all of eternity no place at all.

I have to spend tonight right here.

> (A subtle adjustment of THE MAN's posture suggests a shift in time, no longer on the edge of a sharp precipice.)

There will be no other train. Or maybe there would be. It doesn't matter. When the moment arrived, I could not arrest the functioning of my brain. It had put up every possible obstacle to my following through. I had made my decision not because I had stumbled onto some reason not to act, but because something inside me was desperate to create that reason.

And I listened.

To my… self…

Obviously, I am a Five now.

At least until I am found out. Until the Social Security Administration reclaims my number with a new human being. At which point I will be found out, and my hand will be removed from my body. (Repeating his previous gesture, miming the cut-off hand.)

At which point I will be no more Albert Gardner, but… "Lefty."

Disassembling the device, I bury half of it some fifty yards from the train tracks. I am acting blindly now, not even realizing what I am doing. Obviously I have been thinking of this for some time. Even as I was preparing my assault on the train, my mind was thinking of something else entirely, graciously refusing to inform my "Four" side of the plan.

> (Starting to walk off, upstage, and doubling back.)

And once again, I begin to walk. This time, to the east. I find myself wondering whether there might be an opening for a short order cook in the town of… hmm, Lamar.

To someone, at least, I am "Honey."

That is my identity. The identity that I love. Who cares if I am a Four or a Five or a Three?

It is a stupid criteria.

The other half of the device stays securely in my pocket. *(Again, starting to walk off, upstage...)* I seem to have other plans for it.

(Catching himself, and doubling back once more.) Of course. It is... *evidence!* Evidence that the bloated, self-indulgent Fives... myself included, need to be a little more cautious. Because the Fours...

The Power-Mad, Envious, Sniveling, Reckless, Tyrannical Fours... who had *stolen me from the womb of a Three*, and whose stamp has never been entrusted to my hand, are taking *extraordinary measures, stupid measures*, to destroy, and to claim what had never belonged to them!

It is a stupid criteria.

MUSIC CREEPS IN UNDER.

(Looking at his hand.)

Amazing how it... creeps up on you.

SLIDE SHIFTS to initial "TIMELINE" slide.

(THE MAN turns, and walks off, "East.")

MUSIC SWELLS.

BLACKOUT.

CURTAIN CALL.

FADE LIGHTS TO PRESHOW SETTING.

SLIDE SHIFTS, RESTORING INITIAL "TITLE SLIDE."

Also Available from the TMRT Press!

Molière Than Thou

A Gleefully Giddy Classical One-Man Comedy!

Best of Fringe: Best Adapted Work.   *San Francisco Fringe Festival*

The audience is enthralled… Timothy Mooney is the real deal… A very tight performance indeed, which should be seen by any aspiring actor who wants to tread the boards. *George Psillidies, nytheatre.com*

"Top Ten of 2006" One-of-a-kind… original, weird and seriously funny… one of the most creative and refreshing pieces of classical theatre I've seen in years… Mooney's translations make Molière's 17th century language instantly accessible. His interpretations were crisp, stylized and sang with the comic genius of the playwright's original intent. *Ruth Cartlidge, Chattanooga Pulse*

Mooney is clearly enraptured by the great French playwright… The translations are wonderful… well worth seeing, both for those familiar with the work and those looking for an accessible introduction.
Amy Barratt, Montreal Mirror

Playwright-actor Tim Mooney has become playwright-actor Jean Baptiste Poquelin, a.k.a. Molière… in Mooney's own artful translations… **The humanities are in safe hands this year**.   *San Francisco Bay Guardian*

Molière has never been more accessible… Acrobatic and appealing… Mooney varies his poetic, satirical and vocal tones. He's truly what the French call an *home orchestre* and, as Molière and his characters, the "music" he produces most is laughter.   *Marie J. Kilker, aislesay.com*

★ ★ ★ ★ ½ **Outstanding**... He brings the words of this 17th century playwright to life with his animated performance... At 75 minutes long there were a number of patrons who found the performance too short, because they could have listened to Mr. Mooney all day.   *Ken Gordon, CBC*

What Mooney captures so deftly… is how skilled Molière was in painting scathing portraits of the rich and pompous… the listener can draw all the available pleasure from the splendid speeches penned by the man considered the French Shakespeare.   *Kevin Prokosh, Winnipeg Free Press*

A Molière incarnation… The 75 minutes whiz by unnoticed… I haven't found a single dissatisfied Molière patron. That says something. *Linda Harlos, CBC*

TMRT Press, PO Box 638, Prospect Heights, IL 60070 * www.timmooneyrep.com

With just a costume, a series of wigs and a knack for the language he gives you a good idea of the foolishness, the conniving, the boasting and the masquerading that goes on whenever you see one of Molière's plays…
Clearly Molière lives.   *Elizabeth Maupin, Orlando Sentinel*

A must-see for aspiring drama students and a pleasant experience for the rest of us… Men like Mooney were born for the spotlight and he relishes every character he takes on… every unique voice he takes on fills the room.
                                            The Vue Weekly, Edmonton

Mooney needs only a trunk of costume pieces and his superior histrionics to turn himself into any number of vivid, irreverent, fast-talking characters straight from the pages of the author's greatest works... *I highly recommend* his skilled impersonation of one of the theater's most gifted and important creative spirits.   *Al Krulik, Orlando Weekly*

A brilliant and capable actor, and his presentation of an obsequious entertainer is superb. We all get enough Shakespeare around here, but I say "More Molière!" His innuendo is so much better.   *Carl F. Gauze, Ink 19*

If you're not passionate about Molière now, you may well be at the end of the show: Timothy Mooney's tremendous passion is catchy… truly fits the billing of "*The Best of Molière.*"
                    Marianne Hales Harding – Seattle Fringe Fest Review Rag

Far more vibrant; more full of the lovely ribaldry that Molière would want to be remembered for. Mooney… proves that the rhythm and the life of these works are still very much in the pink.
                    Lee Howard, Seattle Fringe Fest On-line Review

Don Juan speaks like every seedy politician I've ever heard. Scapin's speech detailing how going to court is hell on earth is every bit as relevant as it ever was -- you couldn't alter a syllable. And Tartuffe -- Tartuffe is the same terrifying, monstrous figure that he's always been. It strikes me that one of the reasons that Molière's work has survived is that, sadly, his enemies have outlived him… But what he left us were his vast quantity of words… articulate, brilliant, hilarious, disgusting, despairing. There's a reason he was my hero growing up, enough so that I devoted many years to trying to emulate him. Because *we need his voice. And he's funny as hell.*
                    Minnesota Fringe Blogger, Phillip Low

A very lithe, agile, and physical actor with flawless articulation. He comes off stage in a bound and hops into the seats to involve his audience. And *the Molière is brilliant*. Tim does his own translations… a seamless, fast-paced whole.   *Frank Morlock, Translator/Playwright*

The Big Book of Molière Monologues

Hilarious Performance Pieces From Our Greatest Comic Playwright

(*From the Preface*) "Molière's lines, penned in Classical French over three centuries ago found exuberant reaffirmation in Tim's smooth and stylish English translation... Tim's high esteem and compassion for the greatness and comic genius of Molière is singular… His book of monologues is a masterwork. It represents years of creativity, resolve and follow-through. *I've never seen a better compilation*."
 William Luce, Author, The Belle of Amherst, Barrymore, The Last Flapper

"*Offers more than the title would suggest*. True, there are 160 or so of Molière monologues in new, rhymed iambic pentameter versions by Mooney, taken from Molière's plays... But he also provides plot summaries and contextual information for each piece, as well as an introduction to the life and work of Molière, guides to the performance of classical verse monologues and stopwatch timings of each piece for audition purposes."
 Stage Directions Magazine

A must-read for Molière's fans and neophytes; While having the privilege to see Tim Mooney on stage performing his show *Molière Than Thou* is a wonderfully exhilarating treat, his book of translations is a riveting introduction to Molière and his work… incredibly faithful to the spirit of the plays, requiring much creativity on the part of the translator. Indeed, Mooney was able to put into verse even those works that had been originally written in prose and the effect is outstanding. *Pascale-Anne Brault, DePaul University*

Mr. Mooney has presented *Molière Than Thou*, his performance opus on the French actor/playwright, for many, many years at high schools, colleges, universities, and theaters of all sizes. This newest text is ***the best of his teachings, lectures, and demonstrations in print form***. While there is no substitute for seeing Mr. Mooney perform live, this is certainly a terrific companion piece to his stage work. Mooney's exhaustive research, scholarship, and experience performing the plays of Jean-Baptiste Poquelin has made him one of the world's leading experts on Molière. *The Big Book of Molière Monologues* encapsulates much of that research and scholarship and is invaluable to anyone interested in the "nuts and bolts" of 17th century French Comedy traditions as well as an understanding how these works would have been performed. My best advice: buy this book and then bring Mr. Mooney to your institution or venue to see him bring the book to life!
 Aaron Adair, Southeastern Oklahoma State University

TMRT Press, PO Box 638, Prospect Heights, IL 60070 * www.timmooneyrep.com

FANTASTIC! As an educator, reading it was akin to attending a master class. I immediately went to your site and watched your videos. As a director, I am "chomping at the bit" to work on a Moliere piece again.

James McDonnell, Fine Arts Chair, College of the Sequoias

For those who study and perform the works of Molière and even Big Bill *this book is a must*. It takes you step by step through everything you need to know to become better at the craft, better at the art of performance.

Charley Ault, Director, Players Guild of the Festival Playhouse

I first saw Mr. Mooney perform his one man show, *Molière Than Thou*, at my college in the fall. After his performance had me gripping my sides, I decided that I had to delve further into the author of Molière. I soon found myself enthusiastically reading biographies of him and his plays; I was eager to have more. This book provided me *the perfect accompaniment to my study of Molière* - it has a fabulous collection of some of Molière's most hilarious pieces written creatively for the current actor. The book not only worked well for me with my Molière quest, but also provides a large source of audition pieces. The book covers a broad sweep of Molière's plays and gives descriptions about each character and piece presented... Overall, a wonderful book that presents truly some of the funniest pieces I have read. Enjoy!

Sean B. (On-Line Review)

Tim Mooney has created *an elegantly simplistic highway of understanding*, from the basic description of iambs to the delivery of easily understood, and laughed out loud at, skillfully constructed verse. The key to excellent verse is the simultaneous application of cleverness in a most academic and streetwise manner. Tim does this expertly. Double entendre is a staple by which we all find ourselves thoughtfully smiling or laughing out loud. *Merci, Jean-Baptiste.* Much of Tim's experience shines through in a scholarly manner... *The Big Book* is a must read for any serious French teacher or student of French. To understand Molière is to reach down into our inner being so as to discover and understand ourselves when not fettered by silly political correctness... or assisted by a shrink! Tim's *Big Book* facilitates this in a very American, in your face way. If you don't like Molière or Mooney when you have completed this book, you could not have liked Mad Magazine or the edginess of the old Saturday Night Live (the current one lacks the verve and creativity of the original). So if you are of that ilk, I trust you have read this review before buying it, so my advice is, don't bother, you are incorrigible and not worthy. If however, I've piqued your interest, dive into it... naked, with a glass of red wine and savor it. After you've done that it will be the morrow; so shower, don your clothes and read in earnest! You will be delighted, fulfilled and even a bit smarter in the timeless clever ingenuity of Molière and Mooney's genius manner of bringing this genre to life!   *John Paul Molière, Hume, Virginia*
(Yes, that's right; my name is Molière, it's not a misprint.)

Also Available from the TMRT Press!

Acting at the Speed of Life
Conquering Theatrical Style

A unique 'how to' book offering a refreshing and highly practical approach… No nonsense steps to approach the demands of stylized acting that will be of essential value… Directors and teachers of acting will also find Mooney's book an essential resource… I recommend this exceedingly valuable book which, to be sure, will inspire actors to approach stylized theatre with the spirit of fun and style.   *James Fisher, Theatre Library Association's "Broadside"*

Author Timothy Mooney takes on the challenges of asides, soliloquies and rhetorical speech. He offers tips on memorizing lines, incorporating the "stuff" of historical style, and going beyond naturalism and realism as it suits the playwright's intent. *Nicely done.*   *Stage Directions Magazine*

Not just your average acting book: The book combines a comprehensive understanding of modern "method-based" performance styles with a reflection back to an older system that apprenticed young actors into a troupe, and gave them the basic skills needed to survive as theatre professionals. Powerful and empowering… it's necessary for every serious actor's shelf.
     Dennis Wemm, Glenville State College

A practical, informative and entertaining read! A very "nuts-and-bolts" approach to acting the Classics. His insight into the Shakespearean character alone is worth the price, but he provides useful and thoughtful analysis into Molière, Chekhov, and other playwrights' works as well. I have and would recommend this to the casual or avid theatergoer, the theatre educator, and the performer who desires to know more about how characters are brought to life.
     Aaron Adair, Southeast Oklahoma State University

The hardest-working book in my life of teaching acting to high school students… Results are seen instantaneously… From the basics of memorization to the clearing of the cobwebs surrounding the classics, the book does it all with grace and great humor. The book delivers. I highly recommend it.
     Claudia Haas, Playwright for Youth/Artist in Residence, Twin Cities

Terrific… Replete with incisive, clear-headed accessible advice and information. *In my view it is the clearest and most comprehensive work for the community and student actor written today.*
     Dr. Christian H. Moe, Southern Illinois University

A particular talent to inspire students to explore the classics… One performance with Tim equals a week of teaching and a lifetime of appreciation.   *Michael Stiles, Theatre Teacher Musselman High School*

TMRT Press, PO Box 638, Prospect Heights, IL 60070 * www.timmooneyrep.com

A thunderous success! When, after guiding my cabaret class through your "Exercise," they returned to their songs and took the text out to perform as a monologue, their readings were inspired and wonderful! Their songs came alive with nuance and subtle interpretive freedom. They were humblingly beautiful, startlingly authentic, and persuasively convincing.
Loren F. Salter, Artistic Director and Performance Coach

Wow... what a great text... I participated in the exercise where Mr. Mooney took two young women from the audience and asked them to perform a short dialogue from a Molière play. After a slight adjustment from Mr. Mooney, the two performers lit the room on fire!... This is probably the most accessible approach to classical style that I have ever seen.
Celi Oliveto, Master of Letters/MFA Candidate, Mary Baldwin College

Highly recommended. A treasure trove of tips–useful not only to actors and educators, but also to directors, producers, and writers. The section on Shakespeare alone is worth the price of the book. Mooney's enthusiasm throughout is absolutely contagious.   *V.Z. Daly, Playwright, New York, NY*

This could be the modern manual for the Director and the Actor. Written with the insight of Hagen, Adler, and Spolin… A fun romp, but more than that... a must read!   *Charley Ault, Director, Players Guild of the Festival Playhouse*

The audience who cheered his *Molière than Thou* should appreciate Tim's new book... It goes from basics to advanced-but-de-mystified info on plays by Shakespeare and Molière.   *Marie J. Kilker; Aislesay.com*

The director was loving and laughing at my character and I KNOW your insights contributed to that. I made bold choices--getting the character into my whole body, having FUN!!!   *Betty Anderson, Actress*

One feels the benefits almost instantly; in contrast, when I read some, the vibe is, "you must spend years doing just what I say." Yet when you talk about Shakespeare and pausing too long, for example, just by taking that great insight to heart you can see immediate improvement. These little bits of professional wisdom that you spread throughout are so useful and interesting... You managed to make learning fun.   *Tony Osborne Gonzaga University*

Required summer reading for my Advanced Drama students. The obvious skill and experience you share will be invaluable… "The best acting workshop we never attended."   *Janet Henke, Acting Teacher, Oak Ridge High School*

Communicates with clarity, wisdom and practicality. This text belongs in every theatre artist's bookbag.   *Jeff Barker, Northwestern College*

The advanced students are really hungry for this kind of information and NO other book I've read captures these simple tasks that are so important. I would recommend every acting student to have this book.
Janice Fronczak, University of Nebraska-Kearney

75329958R00035

Made in the USA
Lexington, KY
17 December 2017